Diamonds

Diamonds are the ultimate treasure. Formed millions of years ago by the violent forces that created our planet, these sparkling pebbles are among the oldest objects on earth. Of all the jewels discovered, diamonds are the hardest, most brilliant and most beautiful. They are also very rare and very valuable, symbols of wealth and power. For thousands of years, people have sweated, fought and killed for this "king of gems," with its ice-cold fire.

As well as their everlasting beauty, diamonds have other, more useful qualities, which play an essential part in many modern industries. This book looks at the history, mining and processing of diamonds, and examines both their traditional and modern uses throughout the world. A freelance author for the last ten years, Graham Rickard has written many educational books for children.

Spotlight on
DIAMONDS

Graham Rickard

ROURKE ENTERPRISES INC
Vero Beach, Florida 32964

Cover *A collection of "fancies" – the name for colored diamonds.*
Frontispiece *A beautiful cut and polished diamond.*

Text © 1988 Rourke Enterprises Inc.
PO Box 3328, Vero Beach, Florida 32964

Printed in Italy by G. Canale & C.S.p.A., Turin

Library of Congress Cataloging-in-Publication Data

Rickard, Graham.
    Spotlight on diamonds / Graham Rickard.
      p. cm. — (Spotlight on resources)
    Bibliography: p.
    Includes index.
    Summary: Discusses the mining of diamonds and their processing for industrial use or as jewelry.
    ISBN 0–86592–271–3
    I. Diamonds— Juvenile literature.   [1. Diamonds.]   I. Title.
II. Title: Diamonds.   III. Series.
TS753.R53 1988   87–38302
553.8′2—dc19   CIP
                                 AC

Contents

1. What are diamonds?

Despite their beauty and value, diamonds are simply crystals of carbon, one of the most common chemicals on our planet. Carbon is all around us, from the graphite "lead" in our pencils to the soot in our chimneys. In this form, carbon is dark colored and so soft that graphite is often used like oil, as a lubricant. But, under the extreme forces of heat and pressure that formed the world, this same element was forged into the clear white crystal form of diamonds – the hardest substance in the world.

An eighteenth-century brooch, with four topazes set off by the brilliance of diamonds.

Diamonds occur with several different color tints, but the best-quality stones are pure white and crystal clear, like an icicle in the sun's rays. Most stones are not good enough to be used as gems, and 80 percent of the world's diamonds end up, not in a jeweler's window, but as part of a drill bit or saw blade in modern industry. Even a good-quality diamond looks like nothing more than a glassy pebble when it is first pulled out of the ground, and it needs the skilled eye and steady hand of the diamond cutter to release its beauty, turning the rough stone into a dazzling jewel.

Diamond mining today is a very efficient and highly organized industry. Every year about 5 tons are mined in many countries of the world on all the continents. Rubies may be far more scarce and emeralds more expensive, but the diamond's unique combination of qualities surely makes it the most important of the precious stones.

Above *Sawing a rough diamond across the grain can take several days.*

Below *A layout of rough diamonds, laid out in piles of different sizes and grades.*

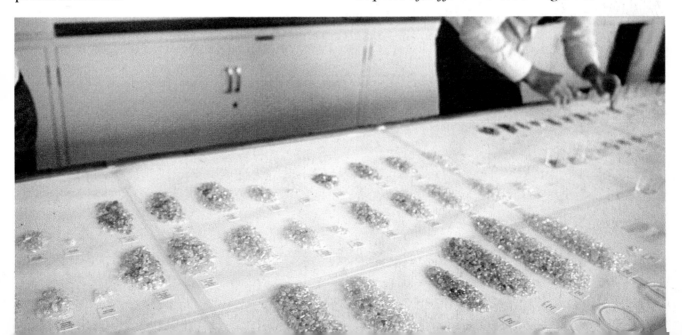

2. How diamonds were formed

Diamonds were formed almost at the same time as the earth itself, millions of years ago. At that time the planet was a fiery ball of molten material, with enormously high temperatures and pressures beneath the gradually cooling

Early diamond mines were little more than enormous holes in the ground. This is the famous "Big Hole" opencast mine at Kimberley, in South Africa.

surface. Patches of carbon, trapped more than a hundred miles beneath the surface of the earth were forced, under these violent conditions, to crystallize into diamonds. Diamonds have been known to explode when they are separated from the surrounding rock, revealing the tremendous stresses within these ancient crystals. These stresses are living proof of the tremendous pressures that first formed the diamonds so long ago.

Diamonds formed in the earth's magma, a dense layer of molten rock nearly 2,000 miles thick, deep beneath the surface. In some places this molten rock was forced to the surface through cracks, in much the same way as volcanoes erupt. This molten rock rose through long thin pipes, up to 75 miles deep. As it cooled, it turned into a rock that is known as kimberlite, or "blue ground." These kimberlite pipes occur in many different parts of the world, and are roughly carrot shaped from top to bottom. Where the pipe reaches the surface it can vary in size from a few feet to a mile wide.

Over the centuries, the cone of kimberlite at the top of the pipe was eroded by the wind, rain and glaciers, exposing the diamonds, which were washed down into river beds or to the ocean This is why many diamonds are found in "alluvial" deposits, in vast gravel beds or on the ocean's floor.

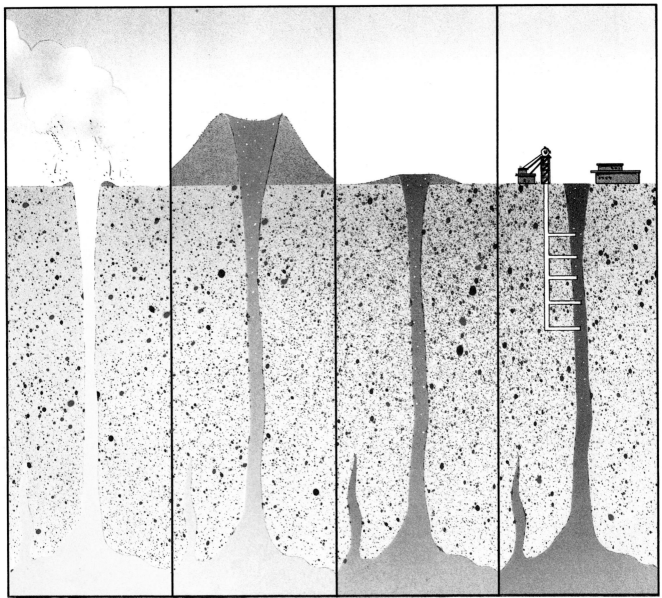

Molten magma containing natural diamonds burst through the earth's crust and cooled into kimberlite pipes. The surface cone was worn away by wind and rain, and many diamonds washed away. The remaining diamonds were mined first from the surface and then from underground.

9

3. The history of diamonds

Diamonds were first discovered more than 2,000 years ago, and from earliest times they were believed to have magical powers. In India they were worn as talismans or lucky charms, to protect the wearer and give him or her strength. Diamonds were greatly prized by the ancient Egyptians, Greeks and Romans, who wrongly believed that diamonds are indestructible – in fact, they can be smashed with a sharp blow from a hammer. The word "diamond" comes from a Greek word *adamas*, meaning invincible, and people thought that by wearing this magic stone, they too would be unconquerable. Even in these early times, people realized how useful diamonds were. Some historians think that the shape of the Egyptian pyramids is based on the diamond crystal, and that the builders must have used diamond-edged tools to cut and shape the massive blocks of stone. Certainly the Romans used diamonds to cut glass.

Diamonds were traded all over Asia and the Middle East, but were unknown in Europe until the Middle Ages when knights brought them back from the Crusades. In the 1600s the East India Company brought diamonds from India to London, from where they were distributed throughout Europe. To this day London, Amsterdam and Antwerp remain centers for trading and cutting diamonds.

Because of their rarity and value, only royalty

An Indian nobleman wearing some of the many large jewels that India once produced.

The British Coronation Regalia, part of the Crown Jewels kept in the Tower of London.

could afford these new jewels, and they became a symbol of power and wealth. Many of these diamonds are still used in crowns and scepters, such as the British Crown Jewels in the Tower of London. King Henri II of France casually wore an enormous diamond in his cap, while the French Emperor Napoleon went into battle with a large stone set into the hilt of his sword, hoping it would bring him victory.

Diamonds were also used as a form of money, because they were an easily portable form of enormous wealth. They were used to pay ransoms, to wage wars, as dowries and as gifts or bribes for royal favors.

4. Diamonds for all

At one time, only kings and nobles had the right to wear diamonds; in the thirteenth century Louis IX, king of France, went so far as to make a law banning all commoners, women and even princesses from wearing these exclusive jewels. The first commoner to break this rule was Agnes Sorel, the beautiful mistress of Charles VII of France, who wore diamonds as a gift from the king.

In Tudor England, the wealthy had a fashionable craze for writing love messages on windowpanes with diamond scribbling rings. Even Queen Elizabeth I is said to have written such messages to one of her favorite courtiers, Sir Walter Raleigh.

Agnes Sorel, the mistress of Charles VII, was the first French commoner to wear diamonds.

Above *A bow-shaped ring set with rubies and diamonds, made in the eighteenth century.*

The ancient Egyptians believed that the *vena amoris* – the vein of love – ran directly from the heart to the third finger of the left hand, while the ancient Greeks thought that the diamond's glow was a reflection of the eternal flame of love. These two traditions were combined in the engagement ring, one of the most popular uses of diamonds in jewelry. In 1477 the first diamond engagement ring was worn by Mary of

During this century the diamond engagement ring has become popular around the world.

Burgundy, who was given the ring by her husband-to-be, Archduke Maximilian of Austria. Until the nineteenth century, only the very wealthy could afford the luxury of such rings as an expression of their love, but today nearly 70 percent of American and British brides receive a diamond ring, and the fashion is becoming popular in other countries. After sixty years of marriage, many of these women receive a second diamond ring from their husbands, on their diamond wedding anniversary.

13

5. Where diamonds are found

Diamonds are now mined on every continent, but this was not always the case. For over 2,000 years India was the main source of diamonds, and many of the world's largest and most famous diamonds were originally from India. Found in the gravel of river beds or embedded in surface rocks, these Indian diamonds were often of good size and quality, but the output was small and resources began to run out as diamonds became more popular in Europe.

The problem was solved by a new and unexpected source in 1725, when gold miners accidentally discovered diamonds in Brazil. A century later a second large deposit was found in another area of the country, and black slaves were driven to breaking point to extract the diamonds as fast as possible. For many years

African slaves are forced to wash diamond deposits in eighteenth-century Brazil.

Brazil was the world's largest source of diamonds, but these resources also began to run out in the nineteenth century.

The center of diamond mining once again moved to another continent – Africa. It began in 1867 when a young boy picked up a shiny stone from the banks of the Orange River. When the pebble proved to be a 21-carat diamond, people began prospecting in other parts of South Africa. Two years later, the great "diamond rush" began after the discovery of the enormous 83-carat "Star of Africa." The famous pipes of diamond-bearing kimberlite in the Kimberley area began to be mined, and by 1872 there were more than 3,500 separate mining claims in the area. South Africa became the world's leading producer, and to this day the entire international diamond trade is controlled by a handful of these original mining companies.

Many other countries in southern Africa, including Zaïre, Namibia, Sierra Leone, Botswana and Tanzania are also important sources of diamonds. The U.S.S.R. has become a very large producer since 1954, when diamonds were discovered near Yakutia, on the Siberian plateau. Australia is the most spectacular newcomer to the scene. One single large deposit, found in 1978 at Smoke Creek near Lake Argyle in the North West Territories, was put into full production in 1985. Within one year of starting operations, it has pushed Australia to the top of the diamond-producers' league.

A mine near Kimberley during the "diamond rush." Prospectors marked out their claims with ropes, and each rope in the picture shows a separate claim.

6. The properties of diamonds

Diamonds may be beautiful, but it is their incredible hardness that makes them unique. Even in our modern world, with its new space-age materials, diamonds are by far the hardest substance known to mankind. No other substance will even scratch the surface of a diamond, which can only be cut and polished by another diamond. Some rare black diamonds are so hard that nothing can cut them. Many times harder than any other precious stone, diamonds are used as a standard to measure the hardness of all other materials. They are not indestructible, however; because of their crystal lattice structure, they can be damaged or smashed by a sharp blow.

*A **diamond cutter** strikes a metal cleaver to split a diamond along its "grain."*

Made of pure carbon, diamonds have the simplest chemical composition of any gem. It is the strong atomic structure of the carbon crystal that makes diamonds so hard. Most natural diamond crystals are octahedrons (eight-sided), but crystals are also found with ten, twelve or twenty-four sides. Whatever the shape, the atoms inside the crystal are bonded together in a very powerful arrangement.

Part of the secret of the beauty of diamonds is their great ability to transmit and reflect light. Even by the light of a single candle, the transparent clarity of a good diamond can make it shine and flash from the other side of a room. As well as brilliance, a diamond has natural "fire" — the name given to its ability to split white light

A rough diamond in its natural shape — an octahedron, like two pyramids joined at their base.

The hardness of a diamond makes it ideal for the stylus of a record player.

into a dazzling blaze of rainbow colors. Diamonds have the highest dispersion index of any natural gem, which explains this "fire," while the "scintillation" or flashing of the stone when it is moved in light is the result of the cutter's skills in creating the jewel's facets.

Diamonds have very low natural friction, allowing them to cut metal and plastics without excessive heat or distortion. They are good conductors of heat, and good electrical insulators. It is their unique hardness and ability to handle light that makes them so beautiful and so useful.

17

7. The value of diamonds

Like snowflakes, no two diamonds are alike, and the value of any one stone depends on its shape, size and quality. Only 20 percent of the world's diamonds are of gem quality, the rest being used in industry. The value of a diamond is determined by four main factors, sometimes known as the four "Cs" – carat-weight, color, clarity and cut.

The size of a diamond is measured by its carat weight. One carat is equal to 0.2 grams. The word originally referred to the seeds of the carob tree, which are very light and uniform in weight, and were once used by diamond merchants in the Middle East as a measure of weight. Large diamonds are rarer and therefore more valuable than small ones, and they are also more beautiful, because they have a larger surface to capture and reflect light. But a good-quality small diamond is worth more than a large stone that is flawed or discolored.

Most natural diamonds have slight tints of color, usually yellowish, but a perfect example is pure icy-white. The best way to judge the color of a diamond is to look at it through its side, against a white background. Some brightly colored stones, known as "fancies," are very expensive collectors' items, and come in many colors, such as green, blue, amber and pink, the rarest being blood-red.

Nearly all diamonds have minor imperfections, called "inclusions," which affect their clarity. These spots, bubbles and lines were formed in the stone when it first crystallized, and are unique to each stone, much like a human fingerprint. Flawless diamonds that show no imperfections to a trained eye are very rare.

Before cutting, some natural diamonds are dull and greasy, and the final beauty and value of a finished jewel depends largely on the cutter's skill. A perfect cut will give the diamond its scintillation, so that it flashes and sparkles as it is moved in the light.

Below *A rough diamond with a large flaw, or inclusion, which affects its clarity.*

Right *The four "Cs" that determine the value of a diamond.*

Cut

How a diamond handles light

The different facets of a round brilliant cut diamond

It is the cut that enables a diamond to make the best use of light.

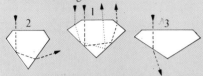

1. When a diamond is cut to good proportions, light is reflected from one facet to another and then dispersed through the top of the stone.

2. If the cut of the diamond is too deep, some light escapes through the opposite side of the pavilion.

3. If the cut is too shallow, light escapes through the pavilion before it can be reflected.

- Table
- Star facet
- Bezel facet ─ Crown
- Upper girdle facet
- Girdle
- Culet
- Pavilion facet ─ Pavilion
- Lower girdle facet

The six most popular shapes of a diamond

Brilliant	Marquise	Pear	Heart	Emerald	Oval

Color

International Color		Grading Systems	
CIBJO		GIA	
EXCEPTIONAL WHITE	+	D	Colorless
RARE WHITE	+	E	Colorless
		F	
		G	
WHITE		H	Near colorless
SLIGHTLY TINTED WHITE		I	Near colorless
		J	
TINTED WHITE		K	Faint yellow
		L	Faint yellow
		M	
		N	
		O	Very light yellow
TINTED COLOR		P	Very light yellow
		Q	
		R	
		S-Z	Light yellow

Clarity

F1	1F	VVS$_1$-VVS$_2$	VS$_1$-VS$_2$	Sl$_1$-Sl$_2$	P$_1$-P$_{11}$-P$_{111}$
(Flawless)	(Internally Flawless – minor surface blemishes)	(Very, very small inclusions)	(Very small inclusions)	(small inclusions)	(Inclusions: visible to the naked eye)

Carat-Weight

0.25 carat   0.50 carat   1.00 carat   1.25 carat   1.50 carat   1.75 carat   2.00 carat   2.50 carat   3.00 carat

8. Early diamond mines

Until fairly recently, all diamonds were mined by digging into the rocks, gravel and sand near rivers. These alluvial diamonds were usually found fairly near the surface, and the digging was much simpler than in modern diamond mines, deep underground.

With no machines, it was very hard manual labor in the early Indian mines, where

After mining, the Kimberlite ore is carried in underground railroad wagons in an African diamond mine.

Slaves working on the alluvial diamond deposits in Brazil.

thousands of men, women and children took part. The men did the heavy digging, while the women and children washed and sieved the sand and gravel to recover the diamonds.

When diamonds were discovered in Brazil, all the hard work was done by slaves, captured on the coasts of Africa and forced to work long hours under terrible conditions. Cruelly oppressed by their white masters, the slaves were lucky to be fed in return for their labors, while the mine owners grew rich from the vast output of diamonds.

When the first diamond-bearing kimberlite pipes were discovered in South Africa in the 1880s, no one realized just how deep they were, because all diamonds had previously come from shallow alluvial deposits. At first the miners used picks and shovels to dig out the kimberlite, and sledge hammers and sieves to break up and sift the rock, before picking out the diamonds by hand. As the mines became ever deeper, the problems increased, and more mechanized methods had to be used. Sacks and barrows, then buckets on ropes were used to haul the stone to the top of the mine. Later, horses and steam engines were used to drive winches, which pulled trolleys to the surface on cables. But these early diamond mines were still really no more than enormous holes in the ground, and some of them are still to be seen in the Kimberley area of South Africa.

Dutoitspan, South Africa, only three years after diamonds were found there.

9. Modern mining methods

Opencast mines are expensive in time and effort. An average of about 250 tons of kimberlite ore has to be mined and processed to recover just one carat of polished diamonds. This explains why diamonds are so expensive, and why modern diamond mines are designed to extract as much kimberlite as quickly and cheaply as possible.

Below *An enormous opencast diamond mine in South Africa.*

Above *Blasting the diamond-bearing rock in an opencast mine.*

All pipe mines start as opencast pits, in which the rock is blasted with explosives, and recovered with large mechanical excavators and dump trucks. This method is efficient only to a depth of 590 feet (180 m), after which the hole becomes too deep and steep for earth-moving machines to operate. One answer is "chambering," a mining technique first used in the 1880s. Large vertical shafts are sunk all around the pipe, and miners extract the kimberlite from horizontal tunnels into the side of the pipe.

A more modern and efficient method is "block caving," which is faster, cheaper and needs fewer miners. A powerful mechanical scraper removes the kimberlite from the pipe, and automatically loads it into waiting trucks in a tunnel underneath. The trucks carry the ore to an underground crushing plant, which breaks it

Drilling holes for explosive charges, deep underground in a South African mine.

into small pieces. This crushed material then drops onto a conveyor belt to the large main shaft, where it is hoisted to the surface for processing to recover the diamonds.

23

10. Alluvial diamonds

Alluvial diamonds are still a very important source of good-quality stones, although the mining methods are very different from those in the pipe mines. In some areas, such as Sierra Leone, the diamonds are still recovered by "hand-panning" as they were in ancient India. The gravel is mixed with water in a pan, and gently swished around to get rid of the water and lighter material, leaving the heavier pebbles and – sometimes – diamonds at the bottom of the pan. This is a very slow and painstaking method, and modern mechanized mining techniques are needed to recover large quantities of diamonds quickly.

One African alluvial deposit is the world's richest supply of gemstones. A stretch of beach 50 miles (80 km) long, it lies in the area between the ocean and the desert on the Atlantic coast of Namibia. After building walls to hold back the surf, a fleet of over 300 special machines are used to scour whole sections of the beach, removing all the sand and gravel for processing. When the miners reach the bedrock, they sweep it clean with brooms, and search among the tiny crevices to find the last few diamonds, before moving on to the next

Prospectors in Sierra Leone pan the river bed by hand using wooden sieves.

Huge dredging plants mine the alluvial diamonds from the seabed, off the coast of Namibia.

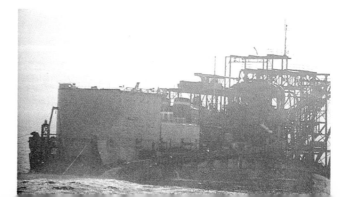

24

section. The Namibian diamond-recovery operation is so large that about 6,000 workers are needed, and a special town, Orangemund, has been built to house them. More than 60 million tons of sand and gravel are removed from the beach each year, to produce about 750 pounds (340 kg) of top-quality gem diamonds.

In a huge operation, part of the Namibian coast has been mined to recover the diamonds.

Some diamonds lie on the seabed, off the Namibian coast, and large ships are used to dredge these deposits, reaping even more of the rich harvest of precious stones.

11. Processing the kimberlite

After the kimberlite has been mined and crushed, the diamonds have to be separated from the vast quantity of waste rock and gravel. This recovery process is long and complicated, and constant checks are needed to ensure that none of the precious stones are thrown away with the waste rock.

The kimberlite is first put into rotary washing pans containing muddy liquid. The diamonds and heavy materials sink, while the lighter particles float to the surface to be skimmed off.

After the kimberlite has been crushed, it is put into rotary washing pans.

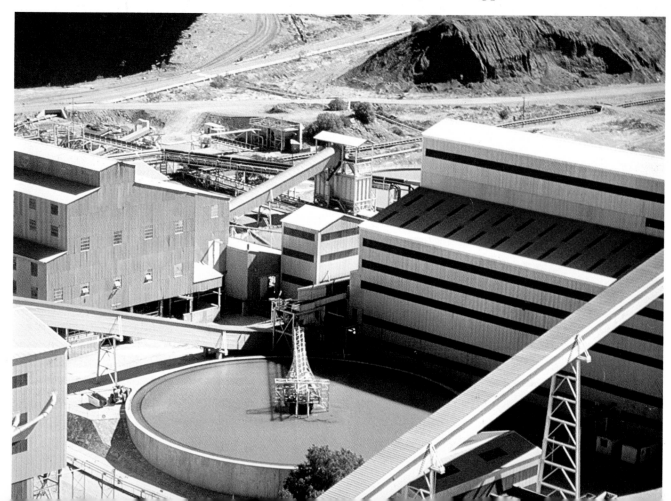

The treatment of South African miners has long been a subject of world concern. This early photograph shows miners being searched as they leave the site, a practice that continues to this day. Most black miners are paid less than their white colleagues, and have to leave their families and homes to live in crowded accommodation provided by the mining companies.

Once the diamond-bearing material has been concentrated, the wet muddy residue is passed on to a large grease belt. Mined diamonds have a natural greasiness that keeps most of their surface dry; when a stream of water is passed across the belt, the diamonds stick to the belt, while the other material is washed away.

One of the diamond crystal's many unique qualities is that it gives off a fluorescence when seen under X-ray light. Modern methods often use X-rays to identify and separate diamonds, which otherwise often look much like any other pebble at this stage.

Despite their unimpressive appearance, these rough diamonds are very valuable. To deter any would-be thief, security is very strict, with high fences, dogs and armed guards to protect the mines and processing plants. Workers and their cars are frequently searched before they leave the site. On the large Namibian alluvial deposits the diamond area is sealed off, to make smuggling that much more difficult.

12. Sorting the diamonds

All rough diamonds go through several stages of sorting and valuing before they are eventually sold for cutting and mounting. The first stage usually takes place at the mining site itself, where the stones are pre-sorted and a provisional value is agreed. Roughly half of all diamonds are useful only for industrial purposes, and the remaining gemstones are sent to sorting offices, like those in Kimberley and Johannesburg, for more careful sorting.

A machine is used for the initial sorting of rough diamonds at Orapa, Botswana.

Most of the world's gem diamonds pass through the headquarters of the Central Selling Organization (CSO) in London, England, where they are carefully examined many times as they are sorted into one of 5,000 or more categories. Sitting at benches, facing north to receive the correct natural light, rows of skilled sorters can pick out a quality stone, even at this rough stage. The 600 workers at the London office sort tens of millions of stones every year, with very little help from machinery.

One of the most important features is the natural shape of the diamond, because this determines the final cut of the finished gem. Workers sort the diamonds into six basic shapes — "stones" (regular shaped crystals), "shapes," "cleavages" (irregular or broken crystals), "macles" (triangular stones), "flats" (thin, flat stones) and "cubes."

These basic shapes are then re-sorted according to size, as their value depends largely on their carat-weight. The stones are also examined for color and clarity, and graded very accurately. Some stones are discovered to have serious flaws and weaknesses, and are set aside as "near-gems" to be used in industry.

Above *Soft natural light is essential for sorting diamonds by hand.*

Below *The six basic shapes of a diamond — stone, shape, cleavage, macle, flat, cube.*

13. The trade in rough diamonds

World supply and world demand for diamonds varies from year to year, so it is important that the price of diamonds is kept fairly stable. Almost the entire world market is controlled by one South African company – De Beers Consoli dated Mines, which also owns the Central Selling Organization (CSO). De Beers cooperates with world governments and other organizations to control the flow of diamonds and keep prices steady by stockpiling the stones when supply exceeds demand.

De Beers and other companies have buying agents and offices in many producing countries, and from here more than 85 percent of diamonds, including Russian stones, pass through the CSO headquarters in London. Diamond trading is a very large and complex business, and the CSO uses the most advanced computerized techniques for recording and

A diamond dealer examines rough stones in Sierra Leone.

controlling their stocks.

The way in which diamonds are sold to customers may seem strange to an outsider. Clients inform the CSO of their requirements, and the company does its best to match their needs with their existing stocks of rough stones, which are then packaged into sealed boxes, or "parcels." Sales, called "sights," are held ten times a year in London, South Africa and Switzerland. At each of these sights, up to 300 buyers attend to receive their parcels although they have never seen the diamonds inside

As part of their monopoly of the world market, De Beers also spends millions of dollars promoting diamonds with worldwide advertising campaigns. Famous slogans, such as "Diamonds Are a Girl's Best Friend," and "A Diamond Is Forever," have opened up profitable new markets. In Japan, for example, the diamond engagement ring is fast becoming as popular as the traditional pearl as a symbol of love.

A buyer examines his "parcel" at a "sight" in the CSO's headquarters.

14. Cutting the diamond

The skilled eye and steady hand of the diamond cutter is needed to bring out the true beauty of any diamond. The flashing fire of a well-cut stone was unknown until modern cutting techniques were developed in the seventeenth century. A Belgian, Louis de Berquem, was the first to cut diamonds geometrically, but it was Vincento Peruzzi, from Venice, who first managed

Right *The stone is carefully marked with India ink before cutting.*

Below *"Bruting" uses one diamond to grind down the rough edges of another.*

to cut all 58 facets of the modern "brilliant" cut. Peruzzi placed 33 facets on the "crown" (the top part of the stone), and 25 on the "pavilion" (the lower part), separated by the wider, angled "girdle." The facets all had fascinating names, such as star, bezel, templet, lozenge, quoin, cross, skew and skilt. The cutting of these facets has to be accurate to produce the "bonfire of light" effect. Light entering the stone is bent and split into the colors of the spectrum by a top facet, reflects from a lower facet, and passes out through yet another top facet.

A diamond cutter first examines the stone very carefully, decides on its final shape, and marks it with India ink. Another diamond is used to make a mark along this line, and the stone is split along its natural grain with a metal cleaver. More often, though, the stone has to be sawed across the grain. A very thin revolving metal blade, its edge coated with diamond powder and olive oil, takes up to two days to saw through a diamond. "Bruting" rounds off the edges of a diamond, and is done on a lathe that holds the stone against another diamond, grinding it down as it spins. The round brilliant is the most popular, but other popular shapes are the marquise, pear, emerald, oval and heart. "Specials," such as Christmas trees, are cut to order.

To finish the stone it is faceted and polished by holding it at different angles against a revolving diamond-coated disk, called a "scaife."

Amsterdam was the traditional world center for diamond cutting, but diamonds are now also cut in Belgium, India, Israel, South Africa and the United States.

Faceting a stone by holding it at a precise angle on a revolving grinding disk.

15. Diamond jewelry

An intricate ribbon brooch, with diamonds and a suspended pearl, made 200 years ago.

Fashions change in jewelry as in everything else, but it is still the engagement ring that provides the biggest market for gem diamonds. But the pure white brilliance of diamonds make them the perfect gemstone for all kinds of jewelry. A large single jewel looks magnificent in a simple setting, while a cluster of tiny diamonds are themselves the perfect setting for a larger colored stone. Precious metals, such as gold and platinum, contrast beautifully with the icy glitter of a diamond, and designers often use these metals to show off any stone to its best advantage.

Any piece of jewelry begins life as a design on a piece of paper. Working from this, the jeweler makes the metal setting, either directly, or cast from a mold. Then the stone is set in place, held by metal claws. The finished piece could be a ring, brooch, earring, pendant, bracelet or necklace, and the price of these articles varies greatly, according to the size and quality of the stone.

In Victorian days, jewelry tended to be large and ornate, with big stones in heavy gold settings that totally enclosed the edge of the diamonds. Tastes began to change when platinum became popular. Platinum is stronger than gold, and allows diamonds to be set in claws, holding the stone away from the mounting, and thus allowing it to catch and reflect

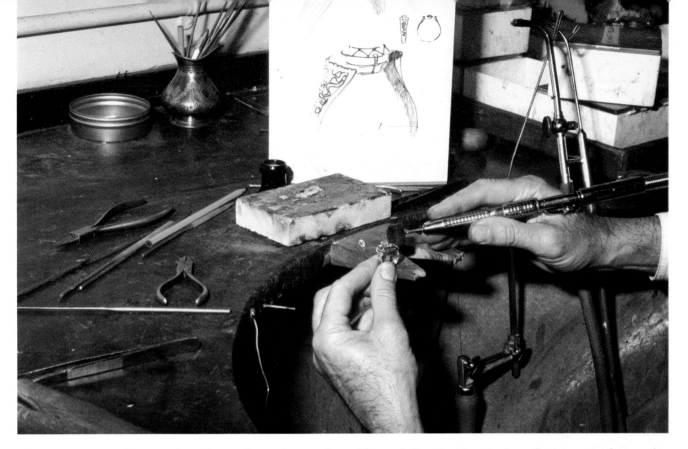

A designer makes a drawing of a piece of jewelry before the jeweler starts work.

Ten of the most popular shapes are shown in this collection of modern diamond rings.

more light. The brilliant-cut solitaire was accepted as the classic cut for rings until the 1920s, when emerald-cut diamonds came into vogue. The following decade saw the fashion for "illusion" rings, which made a small stone look larger by setting it on an oversized metal plate. The modern fashion is for simple designs that best enhance the natural beauty of diamonds. A growing fashion in the United States is for men's diamond jewelry, which now accounts for 10 percent of jewelry sales here.

16. Diamonds in industry

The hardness of the diamond crystal gives it the ability to cut any other material, whether natural or synthetic. Far from the glamorous image of the jeweler's window, over three-quarters of all the world's diamonds end up in factories and workshops. Diamond-edged tools play an essential role in cutting, grinding and polishing the products of modern industry. Diamonds cut faster, last longer, and produce less frictional heat than any other substance. The world's industries use more diamonds every year, as more and more uses are discovered for this most versatile crystal.

Different sizes of diamonds, from the largest crystal to the finest dust, are used for different jobs. Large whole stones are used in drill bits for exploratory oil rigs, both to drill holes and to take core samples for analysis. Smaller crystals are used to tip the grind-wheels that cut and shape metals, concrete and slabs of stone used in the building industry. Diamond-beaded wire quickly cuts large chucks from quarry rock faces, and the chunks are then sliced by diamond-tipped metal bands on a large frame saw.

One of the oldest uses for diamonds is to cut glass. A small diamond, set in a simple holder, is still used by glaziers to score the surface of sheet glass, which then cracks cleanly into two parts. In the modern glass industry, diamonds

Cutting patterns on a glass vase, using a diamond-edged copper wheel.

are used to cut, shape and edge sheet glass into windows, shelves, mirrors and store windows. Glass is very brittle and abrasive, and the diamond crystal is the only material that can cope with the modern high-speed methods of production. Finished glass products, such as tableware, have beautiful decorations cut into them with diamond-tipped tools, and lead crystal glass can be faceted on a diamond-impregnated wheel.

A large diamond-tipped circular saw cuts easily through a solid brick wall. Water is used to cool the blade.

Ground into a fine powder, diamonds are made into a paste for fine polishing processes in many different industries. These abrasive particles are sieved through screens into different sizes, and are used to give a fine finish to metals and many other materials.

17. The useful jewel

Single diamonds are used to cut plastic contact lenses to precise sizes.

As recently as forty years ago, diamond edged industrial tools were still a novelty, but today many modern industries could not survive without them. As well as cutting, grinding and polishing, diamonds also play a large part in many of the latest technologies.

Because they generate very little heat through friction, diamonds can be used to cut such abrasive materials as fiberglass and carbon fiber, which would soon blunt any other cutting edge. This lack of friction also makes diamonds the ideal choice for cutting and shaping plastics and rubber, which are easily burned and distorted by heat.

Diamonds are used extensively in medicine and science, where accuracy is of vital importance. Dentist's drills, for instance, have tiny diamond bits, which drill teeth quickly and painlessly. Eyeglass lenses have to be carefully shaped for each individual, but a diamond takes only two minutes to shape each lens. Even more difficult is the shaping of modern soft plastic contact lenses, but the diamond cutter on the latest automatic machines can perform this delicate task with ease. Small razor-sharp diamond crystals are used by doctors to make the very fine incisions needed for cataract surgery and other eye operations.

Scientists use diamonds to slice thin sections of bone or rock for microscopic examination.

Many scientific instruments, such as microscopes and telescopes, employ lenses cut by diamonds, and this most useful gem is also used to measure hardness and temperature, as a stylus for record players and to transmit the light of laser beams. In the U.S. space mission to Venus in 1978, a "window" of the Pioneer Multiprobe was made of slices of single crystals of diamond, the only material that could stand up to the corrosive gases and high temperatures on the surface of Venus. Modern types of synthetic "thermal" diamonds can withstand even higher temperatures, and are used as die stones, to draw molten metals into extremely accurate electrical wire.

Below *A piece of industrial diamond next to a fine gem quality rough diamond.*

Because diamonds can tolerate high temperatures, detect radiation and remain transparent, a 2-mm (0.08-in) thick, 7-mm (0.3-in) diameter diamond was used in a window on the Galileo Jupiter *spacecraft.*

18. Synthetic diamonds

As with other precious materials, such as gold, people have always dreamed of finding a way of manufacturing diamonds. But until fairly recently it was impossible to simulate the conditions of extreme pressure and temperature that first formed natural diamonds. Early experimenters packed graphite into bullets, which they then fired against a stone wall, in the hope that the carbon would crystallize under the impact. In the 1950s, there was a sudden increase in the demand for industrial-grade diamonds, and the technology was available to provide the necessary conditions for the magical transformation – a pressure of 600,000 atmospheres at 2,552°F (1,400°C).

After top-secret experiments by several different companies throughout the world, in 1955 the General Electric Company finally managed to manufacture the world's first artificial diamonds at their research base in the U.S. Four years later, De Beers managed to do the same in Johannesburg, and the diamond entered a new phase of its long history.

Industrial diamonds contain small amounts of metals and other substances, and usually have strong color tints and inclusions, which make them useless as gems. But they do have

Synthetic industrial diamonds are weighed, prior to being used to tip drill bits.

the all-important hardness, which is the main property of any industrial diamond. In fact, as industrial tools they sometimes have several advantages over natural diamonds. They can be manufactured to exact uniform shapes for particular tasks, and, by adding certain ingredients, manufacturers can produce crystals with special qualities. Synthetic diamonds that can withstand very high temperatures can be used to shape molten metals or to cut the ultra-hard

Industrial core drills are stamped after their diamond tips are replaced.

modern materials that are used to make missile nose cones.

Today, synthetic diamonds of all types and sizes are made to order at centers in Ireland, Sweden, Japan and the United States. Of the 150 million carats of industrial diamonds used every year, 75 percent are synthetic.

41

19. Famous and infamous diamonds

As they are passed from generation to generation, some large diamonds become famous for the part they have played in history. One of the oldest Indian diamonds, the Koh-I-Noor (which means "Mountain of Light") dates back to at least 1304, and was first cut in 1530. It was given to Queen Victoria, who had it recut in 1862, and it now forms part of the Queen Elizabeth Crown in the Tower of London.

At 3,106 carats, the Cullinan still holds the record as the largest diamond ever found. Discovered in South Africa in 1905, the diamond cutter is reputed to have fainted when he successfully cleaved it in 1909. It was eventually cut into nine large jewels and 96 smaller ones. The two largest, the Star of Africa and Cullinan II, can now both be seen in the British Crown Jewels.

The Regent Diamond is smaller, but has a fascinating history. Originally from India, it found its way to Europe, was cut in England and sold to Philippe, Regent of France. As part of the French Crown Jewels it had many adventures during the Revolution of 1789, and was buried and smuggled from one hiding place to another. Today, it is a French national treasure, and can be seen in the Louvre.

The large vivid Blue Hope Diamond also came from India, but it has a much more sinister history. Its owners have suffered a long record of misfortunes, including suicide, murder, accidents, rebellions and madness. The world's largest canary-yellow diamond has a more cheerful reputation and is called the Tiffany Diamond, after the famous New York jewelry store that owns it. When the stone was brought to London in 1986, to celebrate the opening of the company's new store, its breathtaking beauty was the star of the show.

Replicas of the world's most famous and largest gem diamonds.

The Head of the Scepter with Cross, part of the British Crown Jewels, showing the famous Star of Africa diamond.

Facts and figures

WORLD DIAMOND PRODUCTION
(Million metric carats)

	1975	1980	1986 (projected figures)
Tables of the "top ten" producers of natural diamonds show the dramatic changes in world production patterns over ten years and reflect the vastly increased consumption of industrial diamonds.			
Australia	—	—	29.0
Zaïre	17	10.23	20.0
Botswana	2.37	5.1	12.9
U.S.S.R.	12.0	10.85	12.0
South Africa	7.8	8.5	10.1
Namibia	1.74	1.56	0.94
Ghana	2.25	1.2	0.65
Sierra Leone	1.38	0.85	0.4
Angola	0.5	0.3	0.18
Liberia	0.6	0.4	0.14
WORLD TOTAL	48.04	41.18	88.7

Features of Diamonds

Color:
mainly colorless

Chemical constituent:
carbon

Transparency:
totally transparent when cut

Refractive index:
2.42   (accounts for great clarity)

Chemical symbol:
C

Atomic weight:
12.011

Atomic number:
6

Crystal shape:
usually cubic octahedron

Specific gravity: 3.5 grams per cubic centimeter

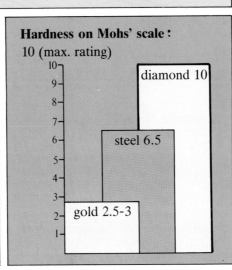

Diamond is 3.5 times heavier than the same volume of water.

Chemical reactivity:
totally inert except at extremely high temperatures, when it will combine with certain metals, such as titanium.

Other qualities:
very high thermal conductivity,
very low electrical conductivity,
very low friction, fairly brittle.

Average size of natural diamond:
0.8 carat

Yield:
one carat diamond for 280 tons of ore (average)

Hardness on Mohs' scale:
10 (max. rating)

diamond 10

steel 6.5

gold 2.5-3

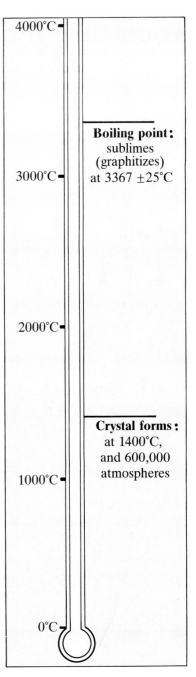

Boiling point:
sublimes (graphitizes) at 3367 ±25°C

Crystal forms:
at 1400°C, and 600,000 atmospheres

4000°C

3000°C

2000°C

1000°C

0°C

Glossary

Abrasive Material such as sand or grit, used for grinding and polishing.

Alluvial Deposits of sand and gravel, washed away by rivers, and found in deep or shallow beds.

Atom The smallest article of an element.

Blue ground Another term for kimberlite, or diamond-bearing ore.

Carat Small unit of weight, equal to 0.2 grams; there are 142 carats in one ounce.

Cleaving Splitting a diamond into two, along its grain.

Crown The top part of a cut diamond.

Die stone Heat-resistant diamond, pierced with an exact-sized hole, for drawing red-hot metal into wire.

Dowry Gift from a bride's family to her new husband.

Facet A flat, polished face on a cut diamond.

Fluorescence Glow given off by some substances when exposed to certain types of light.

Girdle Widest part of cut stone, the angular waist that separates the crown and the pavilion.

Glazier Someone who works with sheets of glass.

Graphite A form of carbon, which is soft and dark-gray in color.

Kimberlite The rock in which natural diamonds are found.

Lubricant Substance, like oil, that reduces friction.

Magma The molten layer beneath the solid surface of the earth.

Pavilion The lower part of a cut diamond.

Pawn To exchange valuable items for money or other goods.

Pipe Carrot-shaped vertical columns of kimberlite.

Solitaire Piece of jewelry having a single gem.

Spectrum The rainbow of colors that make up white light.

Stylus The diamond needle on a record player.

Index

Picture acknowledgments

The author and publishers would like to thank the following for allowing their illustrations to be reproduced in this book: The Bridgeman Art Library 6, 12 (right), 34; De Beers *cover, frontispiece*, 7 (both), 8, 15, 16, 17 (left), 18, 20 (right), 21, 22 (both), 23, 24–5, 26, 28, 29 (both), 31, 32 (both), 33; De Beers Industrial Diamond Division 36, 37, 38, 39 (both); Diamond Information Centre 13, 35 (both); Mary Evans Picture Library 14, 20 (left); HMSO 11, 43 (Crown Copyright); Michael Holford 10; The International Defense and Aid Fund for Southern Africa 27; the Mansell Collection 12 (left); Christine Osborne 30, 42; Graham Rickard 17 (right), 40, 41; Malcolm S. Walker 9, 19, 44–5.